D0507322

Prairie Schooner Book Prize in Poetry | Editor: **Hilda Raz**

University of Nebraska Press | Lincoln and London

NOTES
FOR MY
BODY
Paul Guest # DOUBLE

"For a Woman's Back" is reprinted from *Prairie Schooner* vol. 78, no. 3 (fall 2004) by permission of the University of Nebraska Press. Copyright 2004 by the University of Nebraska Press.

Library of Congress Cataloging-in-Publication Data
Guest, Paul.
  Notes for my body double / Paul Guest.
  p. cm. — (Prairie schooner book prize in poetry)
  ISBN 978-0-8032-6035-1 (pbk. : alk. paper)
  I. Title.
  PS3607.U47N68 2007
  811'.6—dc22   2006101404

Designed and set in Janson by A. Shahan.

Contents

Acknowledgments

The Adirondack Review: "Notes for My Body Double"
American Literary Review: "These Arms of Mine"
The American Poetry Journal: "Love Poem"
Backwards City Review: "Poem in Which I Seek Consolation in the Etymology of a Word"
Blue Mesa Review: "Erasure" and "On Being Asked Who the You Is in My Poems"
Crazyhorse: "From the Black Lagoon," "The Naked," "Plenitude," and "Poem for the National Hobo Association Poetry Contest"
DIAGRAM: "Donald Duck's Lament"
420pus: "How It Won't Be"
The Greensboro Review: "Daydreaming of Ghosts" (vol. 72 [fall 2002])
Gulf Coast: "Popular Romance"
Hayden's Ferry Review: "Psalm in Rain"
Hunger Mountain: "Questions for Godzilla"
In Posse Review: "Perfume"
LIT: "The Cartoonist in Hell" and "Elba"
LitRag: "My Philosophy of Other Lives" and "Resignation"
Lyric: "Beyond Repair," "Negation," "Romance," and "Veneration"
New Orleans Review: "Ptolemaic Sunset"
Octopus: "Apologia"
Passages North: "Hunger" and "The Numbers Are Not In" (vol. 27, no. 1 [winter 2006])
Pebble Lake Review: "Seduction with Entropy"
Poetry: "Lullaby" and "Ode"
Prairie Schooner: "For a Woman's Back"
Slate: "The Invisible Man Looks into a Mirror" and "Water"

The Southern Review: "Questions for Silence" and "Such as Myself" (vol. 42, no. 4, pp. 700-703)
Swink: "Minus"
Verse: "The God of Neglect, Overheard"
West Branch: "At Last," "Exit Interview," "Nothing"
Willow Springs: "History"

My thanks to Rodney Jones, Rick Jackson, Lucia Perillo, Bob Hicok, Ed Brunner, Allison Joseph, Joel Brouwer, Bruce Smith, Victoria Chang, Aimee Nezhukumatathil, Cynthia Roth, Matt Guenette, Adrian Matejka, Stacey Brown, Brett Griffiths, Ander Monson, Ted Worozbyt, Sophia Kartsonis, C. Dale Young, Oliver de la Paz, Melissa McCool, Suzanne Frischkorn, Jeanine Hall Gailey, Amy Blache, Mark Womack, Chris Kerley, Bradley Paul, Karri Paul, Laurel Snyder, Betsy Taylor, Chad Davidson, Erica Bernheim, Jennifer Weathers, Heather Ryan, Ruth Ann Daugherty, Stephanie Walker, and Eliot Khalil Wilson.

Notes For My Body Double

Nothing

Between Buck Owens and Vivaldi what's left
to listen to but the stars, so I do, dialing
the radio down to indeterminate static,
what I always thought was absence, an aria
of sizzling nothingness. Instead
it's the Milky Way radiating arrhythmia
all the way back. It's gossip
of the vacuum. That nothing has never been
truly nothing is why I believe,
even still, in love. Beside two rivers
I have lived nearly all my life
and these beneath one sky
muttering its endless alphabet of sine waves.
Jupiter with its flock of moons
and the stone from which we hope
to squeeze one drop of water,
red Mars pulsing in the blank field of night—
I've wanted to leave Earth
behind, gravity's orphan at last,
but not Earth with its two good seasons and two bad
and not its angel-winged clams
luminous in the mud bed of a river
so distant from me
I can't remember where
that water is, except that I've dreamed it,
except that in it I sank
all the way down.

[handwritten margin note, right] Love this image it's so clear and apt – but the word sizzling is a bit off.

[handwritten margin note, left] Water & static, this is the exhale of the universe – breathing energy out to one day breathe it all in again.

I

Plenitude

That boy in the snowy late light
midnight TV gives the skin, blue then
dark then blue, is me. With my mind
shaped like a finger, I point
him out. This is before he will point
a borrowed bike downhill
and touch me in return. This, too, is before
rushing home in rain, through
woods, stopping in a clearing of clouds
and canopy to note moon
like milk on my skin, in the water white
and pebbled, for the first time
in my life. I called it home, the apartment
we would love in after class
and there she waited while I drowned
in my clothes, in that light
bouncing earthward from the sun a world
away. This is before I fell.
This is before I swallowed back
a new species of emotion
I'd never known to live within
my chest, before I said
not a word to her that suggested I might
go away and go unmissed.
This is before I fled. This is before
I hung in the elevator's throat
and waited for the world
to catch back up, for the world to spit back
lost time. This is before

I lost a friend to the vacuum of his blood,
the blown veins leading
back to his heart. This is before
I loved three times. This is before
I feared all day to lose
the last, my heart pulsing like a lead cloud.
This is before. Curled
and in a clot, before long he'll sleep.
He'll rehearse another
life. All night long I wait and I watch.
One by one I write down
what he dreams.

Elba

When she tells me her name I'm thinking
of Napoleon's exile there. Of his hand
in paintings, oddly tucked away,
and the vague memory that it meant
something, once. I'm thinking
then of Bugs Bunny aping Bonaparte
and how as a child I laughed
but did not know the thousands dead
in his name. I'm thinking
not at all what she would like
kneeling there in the aisle of this plane
when she asks if I was born
this way, and who in Chicago takes care
of me, a wife, a girlfriend—
she knows one or the other is in my life.
When I tell her which two
white rings of bone in my neck
are fused, wired, made one,
I can see her ardor marry grief
and <u>I want to save her</u> ⟩ Save her from the path
<u>from my life. I tell her</u> ⟩— of caring.
that some now think Napoleon died
of a hormonal disease
slowly making of him a woman,
his body white, smooth, hairless,
with breasts a physician thought beautiful,
and though she smiles
<u>I can't tell which story she no longer</u>
<u>wants to know</u>.

On Being Asked Who the You Is in My Poems

You are always eighteen or married
or both, carrying inside you
a surgeon or a singer growing
away from you like a little cloud,
and you have just escaped
from the leprosarium hidden
beyond the horizon's lead smudge,
slinking through damp kudzu
to rap at my window
in the slowly sprawling darkness,
in the sodden green glow
of these two nights, mine
and yours. Or you've retired
from a secret life,
the oath sworn upon your bleeding thumb
now broken. The petal,
a curled pink that fell
and boiled in the black mirror of my coffee,
for a moment today was you
just as you were the bone of a thin girl's hip
swimming beneath her
skin like a fish.
Limbless girl
bowling via surrogate
while a jukebox ate through change,
your smile
once broke the earth open like a bone
ribboned with silk red
marrow. In the smoke rank air

[handwritten marginalia:]

Celia —
had to Face North
she walkes up at
night - Feeling that
she's Facing the
wrong direction.
If she fell
asleep not Knowing
what direction
she was headed,
she'd wake up
across the bed.

Walkes up —
this is the
wrong
direction —
but I
don't know
what that
means.

cool color.

5

all the world did
was turn and turning
away I began to keep your secrets like my own.

Questions for Godzilla

What of the atom's split heart we made
for you and the godly flash-bang wrath,
the anguished song, the clawed gait,
the zipper by which one of us slips into
and puts you on, your death we dangle
like a carrot, your stunted son mewling
always, your ragged arch foes,
your bed in rock, in magma, in thick sea slime,
our fascination still, our morbid heart,
our scattering like leaves, our blood
that once was horrible, a Technicolor ichor,
what of the glowing spine,
what of the toy stings of stock footage flames,
what of the jets you swatted dead
from the air with unmistakable joy,
you of the plastic-leather, pebbled Pleistocene flesh,
you of the palsied fury, you
of the put-upon by dissemblers and disturbers,
you, what of the life burned
so cheaply into celluloid we are charmed,
what of autumn, what of the earth
we took you from, what of the sky's wounded throb,
the sallow child darkened
in your shadow, what of those thousand fates
cut in coiling ribbons
to the floor, what of the heaven they hoped on
that glowed like your breath,
that sang only before you came,

that fell quiet like a feather,
what of the shouted orders,
the dread retreat, the fall of a world built to scale,
what is pain to you?

The Invisible Man Looks into a Mirror

Maybe you wake up knotted in your bedclothes
and what you thought your life was, it isn't:

and whatever that was you're forgetting anyway.
A lifetime peels away like a wet bandage.

Your first true kiss is now vapor. Ditto, the first
divorce. The first bone you broke.

Your last bicycle ride. Your first ambulance.
In that gummy dawn between sleep

and this cruelty, you aren't so much a person
as you are litter. Even your bones knock

fearfully, as if they had been strolling
along in liquid moonlight with blood red roses

in their lapels, before being set upon
by a mob of animate mallets, clubs and blackjacks,

before waking in the foreign land
of your flesh. No one here speaks right.

Nice
line

No one here sells the map of all your memories.
Maybe the scratching you hear

at the window is not a tree's tubercular branch,
a nest of jays in the elbow's crook,

all of them starved and singing thin agony—
maybe what you hear at the edge of all

is some larger hunger, a were-beast,
matted with clots of fur, hunched and snuffling.

And maybe not. Already you seem
to yourself utterly soluble, like water in water.

Beyond Repair

[handwritten: His titles are pretty cool metaphors]

All the glass things my hands couldn't abide.
A spider's web. The lampshade you loved.
The Sphinx's nose and the arms of Venus,
All Pompeii and Pisa's slack tower,
[handwritten: things that cannot be fixed]
lashed to the earth. *The Magnificent Ambersons'*
last reel. Our life together. My neck.
The damp matchstick I prayed
would flare. Coaster brakes
I hated and the ancient, rheumy tire exploding air.
My arms. My jaw. A big toe.
The firefly I clapped my hands around
only to smear its summer light
upon a rock. My life's cruelty.
My heart's love, sinking, darker
than imagined dark. The scar that still scabs.
The pennies we placed before trains.
The limbs I lost in some other life; happiness
in another. The past. The ineffable curve
of flesh beneath black silk, My belief in heaven.
[handwritten: How is this broken?]
My credit rating. My sand castle.
The snow I kept for you. Hatchwork
of ink that might have been a bird
had I talent. The tape you unspooled in a fit.
Energy and strength. Right
words. Outrage. An end to kindness.
The waxwing's crushed head.
The list I make in bed, waiting—.
The star that died. The free-floating bone.
Your face in the mirror.
Just a song. The shards I forgot. My own, my blood.

Minus

The phone is never for me except for when it is
and so most days I ignore its digital trill
before someone apologizes to the air
for dropping my blood to the floor,
could I please entrust one more vial
to their care. Or it's the synthetic coo
of a woman I almost believe
could consolidate my vertiginous debt
and more, <u>dragging the vacuum</u>   *— utterly empty.*
<u>of my heart</u> across the twin Alps of the fiscal
and the erotic. But her voice ends
and standing here in the hall
I'm amazed and frozen
cool pair
of words.
by the <u>deep drift</u> of longing sweeping higher
than I was aware. Until this
moment, I had bought many things
I had no need of: the pogo stick
rusting mercifully somewhere cool and dark,
its wheezing ascent grounded;
the ouija board that never whispered at all
of the distant dead; the iguana
whose tail grew black and necrotic
and hardly noticed the amputation
with a steak knife made of space-age materials.
And now I want whatever it is
she was hired to make me want—
I will spend more than I have
so that she will be programmed to return
to the <u>Capistrano of my ears</u>
<u>like a helpless bird</u>. I will burn

dollar bills because it's easier than pennies.
I will fall like Frank Bland fell,
unlucky in name and life,
into a vat of paint thinner
and fight for his life with mine
as we burn away. To the world,
I will open my wallet like a cadaver is opened
and forgive what I'm owed.

History

Manners forbid, or should forbid,
that I write about secret
pleasures, the end of the day and alone, you
in a dark home, lamps and wine
burning together. If there is music,
it thrums like wires in a wall,
and if there is no music, the distant cars hum
a traveling song. And this
is the moment to which my mind
sings: you putting aside the phone
as your hands perform
the perfunctory unclasping of your plain bra.
In that breath, the day's true
end and in that end, the night
beginning, like the moon cactus, at last
to open. And wherever you settle
like this darkness
or these clouds—
on a swaybacked couch,
on a furrowed bed,
wherever you rest
there is a naked ease. Even
in the water of your ancient
tub, lead walled, claw-footed,
like the one launched a mile
outside Pompeii's walls
on that last day, even
in that body of water your body
resists history, resists a final telling.
Forgive me each word.
All that was yours, I imagined was mine.

The ease
& one with
the other.

14

Psalm in Rain

[handwritten margin note: Above / & / dreary]

Leaking hemlock, the clouds come and cold
as death, the rain with them,

the drops fat and hard like cat's eye marbles.
And distance is all the world.

At once in this wetness, the earth bears up
against the storm's static frottage,

taking from me the bit of warmth I keep:
no more than an acolyte's flame

and frail as a ghost, as I was in the days
before these when I could lift up

a burning thing for others to see,
and myself was not what burned

in the grip of others, who loved me,
who conspired with me against so much

oppressive matter. It's wrong,
it must be, to think of the earth

this way: convulsive ball of salt
careening around the sun,

for in my better moments I love it—
the good sense of the living.

And if angels hate us from on high,
let them turn their sour faces

away: I haven't missed them,
and hardly long to join them

in throes of a thousand hosannas.
O God, once we thought

it was your shoulder against
the wheel of the sun,

and your flesh burning in the sky—
the work, the lifting,

of time itself. And then
we knew better. Drowned in air,

if I disturb space at all,
I can't feel it

and the cars sluicing by
are full of warmth and a song

that is not mine
fades and is faint and falls from me.

Romance

Of course, the stars seem nothing like wax
fruit in their orbits and the moon's gloss

is not romantic but terrifying, arid and deep
with alien dust, but I can't help

dressing the world other than it is, tonight.
How red your hair. How cool all this

air. How quiet the dogs grow in their dreams—
but you have never been here. No

hollow of your body dents the mattress
where I lie. All that you are is blue fire

in the earpiece of the phone; all
that the fat wasps ticking the window's scum

are is pain forestalled. I've fretted
for days the smallest things I can:

old comic books so fragrant with time
they lift like spice; a broken sprout beside

the mailbox, yellowing with my grief;
and every bird that has discovered me

no quick study but a throat full of molasses.
I know I'll dream you again

hollowing out with a spoon
some fruit that incandesces

into a star. And nothing will be gained,
locked in a scalding light,

in that moment, in that kitchen stocked
with food going bad, out

of sight.

Negation

I was not your father in his hour of vigil
or insomnia, his shadow joining yours
where you slept; I was not the raw red
of your mother's hands imparting clean
to the sink's burden of dishes. And,
I was not what I had been, once.
Love is grief is not what the morning gave
to your mother's mouth, not
exactly, but it must do. Through that month
you passed like pain; where
you were, a hayseed's dream orbit:
Texas, Kentucky, Tennessee—
and me in Alabama, Dantean in its visions
of hell. I did not dream
of the crowd's eternal hurrah here
or the white elbow of love
linked in mine. Beneath August sky in April,
I did not linger. I thought
of the freshly severed head
a cat once left at my door like a gift or boon—
for days I couldn't touch
such a small thing, its life
surgically pruned from its rabbitish future,
and by other ways I went
not thinking to place in dirt the cap of its dreams.
I did not think of where
it went when it did, only felt
relief rise in my chest like a carnation.
To the vapor of the window I sang a low song.

No, I didn't wait for you
or sleep much at all
or raise one hope like a rag to wipe my lost face.

At Last

All day I wanted, I ached, to tell
you of the rabbit dead in the road
and how the whole day I marked
time with its evisceration—
if at first I had touched its flank
or its sleek ears tucked back,
I would have taken the last measure
of its warmth. The ghost
of its abortive bound would be near.
And later when its torso
began to show, when its pelt was peeled
and its innards unspooled,
I didn't grieve. Flies had come
and in their noise, in their work,
they glittered. The flesh
seemed to sink with the sun
and I thought to tell you
that night at the door,
taking whatever you held
into my arms, *at last I've kept*
vigil over something,
over ruin, come see, come see, come see.
In the cuff of the wind
white petals sloughed
from the branches of the gnarled dogwood,
the tree I was taught
Christ's cross was cut from.
If once I believed
in so much holy ruin,
there was none to be found there.

And this was right.
In the matted entrails
of the slaughtered,
whoever thought to know the future
in the slick, wet coils
never saw me keeping watch
in the failing light
for the dead to vanish and you to appear.

The Naked

I have tried to find in me some true line
or apt angle, tried with the searing

exactitude of the x-ray, and all I found
were bones. And this can be no surprise

to the naked, who never can shrug
off twistedness, as last night,

rolled from the shower and past
a mirror, I saw what I am and what

a child's broken neck makes
of the future. Nothing so different

than what I might have known
in that densely starred sky

we know as the all of otherwise—
there where every atom

of every love I might have known
was not snuffed out

between the gaunt thumb and finger
of God. And there

my hips reflected don't seem
a mess. There, my hands

fold perfectly a plane from paper
and hurl it to the wind.

Sleep, there, beside her
happened. A flower burned like a fuse.

The rain drew back
before me, cowed, all

the clouds above held
like the breath of someone falling.

Daydreaming of Ghosts

Were I to look outside my window and write
down the rain-slick frames of bikes in racks,

the chains coiled like robotic innards,
the wheels large enough to bear my grudge

against the earth, I'd stop: nothing
then could stop me from seeing

the world as I'd make it. Runaway train
pulling a thousand tons of want

beneath the night's speckled eggshell,
I'd be a kind of monster,

the sort of beast who would find
a girl setting daffodils afloat

on the flat, still, glassy water,
and thinking her perfectly a flower

lift her to heaven by lowering her.
And no one could ever forgive this,

nor should they think to, rising
with their pitchforks and torches crackling

like bones, pounding on the bolted door,
demanding my surrender,

my head, my home in flames,
the ground ashy then haunted with salt—

the way certain memories intrude
upon whole days, voiding

the certain beauty of one magnolia
after another. And who would rush

at the last instant and too late
to my defense, my half howl

to the moon dropping with me
from the cliff's edge into a sea like milk?

The God of Neglect, Overheard

O hearts fat with custard, and sweet,
forgive that I move at all

and signal my coming with rain:
forgive the rusted rasp

of all things: the venom-wet wasp
nesting in newspaper,

tenant of scabrous ink;
the starved blur

of the bird pecking nothing
upon the ground, singing

suet and sugar-water, worm and dust.
Were I to forget you

the world would fatten
and the hinges swing free;

rust in rills would run
from where you stood,

shocked still by dawn.
O mouths rimmed in blood,

if I left you
I would return to feed you

black hanks of kelp
from each fist. And again

you would lose the whole
of what was gained

those days I swam away from you
like an echo, dead

to your ears and never
to return, this tipper

of urns and master of mold,
this god of the slack

figure and swollen belly—
O lambs, O marrow melting like wax.

From the Black Lagoon

From shallow water the deep shimmer came.
In black and white, in three dimensions,
in a blurry sweep before our goggling eyes,

the creature from the Black Lagoon
shambled stiffly up from the brackish pool,
draped in epaulettes of black-green kelp,

and snatched from sun-warm reverie
the blonde and helpless bather for his bride.
Down to his sad underworld he sluiced,

with her horror in tow, writhing,
full of drowned scream, her hair streaming.
In the crook of his rubber elbow,

he held her with a webbed, inhuman, paddling hand—
and if she was saved, returned to air,
wrapped wordlessly in a towel

against the coldness of shock,
I can't remember, and begin here to guess.
After long struggles in a slant light,

after the raking of his claws
through the flesh of would-be heroes,
after chaining her bare ankle

to the bone-littered floor of his homely grotto,
after swimming off in grace
to meet men who wanted her back,

who would pierce him again
and again with the long barbs of harpoons,
after all this, beyond air,

she would be saved, and come to love
in the agony of rising
the man who pushed water from her lungs.

And in my imagination this is fine—
an inspiration, this breathing in to,
this wondrous salvation mired in dreck—

I'm grateful for it, though I forget
myself, that I was ever there
with hundreds treading water together

to watch with cheap cardboard glasses
perhaps not these scenes,
not exactly, I'm sure, but roughly akin,

projected on old canvas that fluttered
like a sail in summer wind.
And to turn for a while from the film

was to look back upon a sea
of strangers in water to their waists,
if tall, to their breasts or necks

if not, all of them in that strange dark
seeing through red and blue lenses
the creature swimming toward them,

up from that fatal depth, a dream
of loneliness, impossible to kill,
the heart in the throat rising like a scream.

How It Won't Be

In glorious black and white with the surge
of salt foam racing around the isle
of our twining bodies. Punctuated
by fireworks, by rain, by snow,
by safely errant trajectories
of bullets and tanks and strafing biplanes
in the star-freckled sky. Aswoon,
afloat, afire, astride, aloft, akimbo,
none of these, no. Not
in the orbit of the earth or its molten core,
where gravity dissipates
at the last, where the seed
of the world floats within itself
far from the eyes
of you and me. In the largest eyes ever,
the goggling gimlets
of the architeuthis
as we sink in the inkwell dark
of the blind ocean.
As extras in the cast of *Yog the Space Amoeba*,
mouthing Japanese
we never before knew,
our fear real, the danger fake,
each building burnt
like a cheap cigarette,
down to an ashen stub, down to the loveless earth
where you say to me
we must run or die.

Seduction with Entropy

If you think I'm honest, speak to me
when it's night. I'll say anything
when my face is blank like a moon.
But not the scarred one stirring
the tide. A better moon, a sphere
of burnished bone. To that sky,
I'll lie through the open gate
of my teeth. I'll turn you
to tender gooseflesh. I'll serve
you on the table of your hidden
hunger. I'll find it the way
rain finds my roof each night
you take yourself away
to that land in which you are only
yourself. I began this
long ago, I'll say. It's precious like silk,
I'll whisper like the clock.
Like the clock, let us be
imperceptibly slowed,
let us watch the water never
boil. Darling, beyond
the loneliness of the moon
is dust, is the pulsar's faltering signal,
the only remainder
of what once could set fire to fire.
Nothing we know
will ever in return know us
for what we were
and how we burned.

If nothing else
I say is true,
let the ashes finally fall, we'll call it mercy.

Veneration

Mummified, you, with your nail bandaged, split
from the underside up, revealed no kinetic chef,
just hunger for one more thing I didn't know—
Indian eggplant? I try to imagine how
the blade found meat not meant for its edge.
Clumsiness, you say—
the freakish alignment of quarks and the wild nothing
of neutrinos, all tallying up a starry end
for you. Nothing so romantic
as a piano twirling from a frayed umbilical
above you, grateful in shade. The thousand agonies
of Three Stooges flicks might not ding
or leave a dint in you, yet your blood slips
loose for this disappointing plant,
hardly regal, its dermis to the touch so like our own.
And today I read how the Mississippi
flows away from itself at three miles an hour—
I had never given water's speed
a moment's time, not when it was a calm murmur,
but I thought then, walking home,
fixing in my mind this greenness pushing up from earth
like veneration, I thought then
to tell you how your blood could best a mighty river.

Apologia

The homework swallowed the dog
and I left my burdened wallet
in my other life, in my other car,
which is a Soyuz, Russian
in only the ways that matter.
And what those ways are,
well, I forget. It is a good thing
the constellation of atoms
you recognize as me
has not yet sought to diverge,
to divorce itself
from this idea I keep having
about being alive. That:
it's lucky my lungs fill up with air
each morning like little
buckets brought to the pebbled rim of the river
by a girl who thinks
about devotion
the slow way back to everyone,
to endless thirst.
And that girl is you,
though you'll bristle
at the very notion,
and rightly so:
what sense does it make to speak
of heartbreak
for even a moment
in this world cluttered with warehouses
of cheap peanut butter,
skinned with thin puddles of oil,

what sense does it make
to ask you
why I'm constantly dreaming I'm late
to your life? What sense
is there anywhere?
In what tree sings the bird
to which I spent all spring
teaching it the mimicry
of your sweet laugh,
but not the burr of your anger,
like a stone,
like a blade,
and not the worried ways of your tired voice.
It's late again
and the moon
teaches me stealth
and borrowed light
and lowered gravity
and before sleep
let me say
my apologies
like a prayer,
to you,
let me miss you as long as I'm alive.

In Praise of the Defective

When the best of it is prized from the dung
of the Sumatran common palm civet,
sweetened like a cherry in the gut
of this little island cat, I feel better
about not drinking coffee, sipping instead sweet
tea crude as a hammer. I feel
better that I never read much
Tolstoy, stopped at the bulwark of so much
French. I should begin
a second life. I should not dream
of my macrobiotic afterlife
in which I am what I do not eat
and the animals I loved enough
to eat grass, to pretend one thing was another,
purr and sing and chirp
sweet hosannas outside my bedroom window
where sometimes we made
love but never continuances
of our selves which we'd name
Hank or Emily while saving up for Harvard.
I feel better that none of me
works well at all,
that for twenty years the fog
has never lifted
from the landscape I mean to cease defiling
someday. Thank you
cards I should have mailed
and gifts given
and favors repaid with crippling interest

I grow to love
the way I once loved
shame. What will I do with my days
now that my nights
are sublimely alone
and how will I make use of this wound
I carried like a map
so that I would never, never
lose you?

Exit Interview

This is about failure but let's pretend
it's the rain that fixes us here
stamping our feet in this gulag
of a month. Let's pretend the moon
isn't the sky's scar tissue.
Let's pretend the artifact
of our breath will remain
obedient, not like a dog
licking the salt
from your hands, but like
a robot or a butler,
or in a better world than this one,
a robot butler. Let's say
it was summer
and the world
became a lurid green
and all we could
do to survive was darn the socks of tyrants
in a cave beside
the green murmur of the sea.
What would it mean
turning to you
in the night
disguised in the milk light of the moon?
To your throat
I would press
my lips like a voided stamp.
You could never return me.

If this life is
the only one,
it will not be so hard to love ashes before salt.
To always ache.

Resignation

Because the air is peppered with the sallow seed
of the grass and I sneeze like a lathered beast,
because the air, for all its jay blue, has failed

to catch the rain and keep me dry as matchsticks,
because of the air's tacit approval of clouds,
(though they may seem to be airy castles

or cotton-white plumes of a dragon's breath)
I have spent too much of my life
unsuitably pale, because of its feckless faith.

So I take my leave of the air.
I divorce myself of the peregrine's span.
I bundle in inky newsprint the soft pink glow of my lungs

and wait, sipping amber tea, here
in the air to which I no longer speak
though it feathers my skin like a monarch,

though it confesses the litany
of its secret betrayal like a nerveless lover.
I wait to grow gills and fins,

a lateral line to soon light
the deep dark of my path. I wait
to lose the lids of my eyes. To go, to dart, to slosh.

The Cartoonist in Hell

Jonny Quest, no one remembers you. Sad,
but I've asked. No one likes to dwell
in the genial weather of befuddlement
for very long so I change the subject
better than any mercury-addled alchemist ever
and say *my belt buckle is in retrograde*
or *if only I could knit for you*
a sweater made of one spider's silk
then you would consent. But,
it's a lonely light I hide like an injured
thing. The rust-colored kids
stampede like flame along cartoon gunpowder.
That's their sky but not mine
as they pelt the hanging hive
with rocks, the bees' industrious drone
spilling out. Tonight, maybe,
I'll dream of each comb's cataract
of honey. Or the red-haired
girl I lost. Both amount to the same sick
sweetness. Tonight, maybe,
I'll tweeze her name
from my life at last
and to the clockface,
irradiated and sickly,
keeping count like a stunted child,
I won't confess the clinical histories
of the stars or admire
the misknit bones of the denuded dawn.
I drew this on a map
I never needed,

I drew this vacant swirl of lines
and later added eyes
so that something might blink back for me.

My Philosophy of Other Lives

Of all my imagined, diabolical anti-selves,
of all the stunted needlers and stark oglers,
of all the speed-sick throttlers and scabbed
denizens of the night, of all the sepia-soaked
lycanthropes and lumbering, green, aphasiac dead,
of all those blooded with derring-do,
of all those itching for wrongness,
of all those hanging by one more snapped neck,
of the dread, burned ones, the vanished,
the halved, the spilled, the broken, numb and blind ones,
of the ones whose last words
to the air even I do not know,
of the transparent, the invidious and the benighted,
the ones by a word scalded,
the ones who stepped from paintings,
the scribblers by candle
of odes and epodes to their dashed and slanted loves,
of tomorrow's appetites, of the larkspur,
of the moldering world,
of you who I loved and failed
and the slack apologies between,
of so much rust,
of the line drooping with clothes,
of the ditch brimming with rain
and the book, swollen and deformed,
there at the clear bottom
that no one now will read—
of those words, that story,
that beginning and end,
of those ruined lives
let my song shiver like struck piano wire.

Donald Duck's Lament

All those years an avatar of rage and fury.
My feathers gone in fits until I'm ink
and nubbled flesh, pink. A poor meal,
by my naked look. A long knife in a dark
drawer, my heart would open me
in an instant, a wet moment, nightmare.
Maybe then I'd begin to know
what sweetness is, if it's a revenge
upon the earth for all its grubbing and lack,
its insistence upon flight. And
for the denial of wings, I hate what god
made me hands. I make all fists.
Alone, I would have been fine.
Filled my days with model trains
and trees whittled down,
lowered my face into miniature smoke
rising from the locomotive,
at once acrid and sweet—
inhaling it all, a heaven to hold forever.
Or, a picnic, on a green hill.
Autumn sun, sandwiches stacked high,
and who I could love
with me on a red gingham blanket,
both of us fattened by time.
You would think a bone stoppered my throat
for how I talk, ridiculous clot
of babble and gurgle, impediment
as dreamed by the idiot or obvious—
and then writ large, screamed out
so no one with ears could ever miss me.

And for all that, who'd listen
but to the stilted music I make,
father of laughs, forever waiting
for the wooden mallet to come down,
tear open my mind, paint red
the whole world I looked on at dawn,
for a moment, with faint joy?
Call me a wrung-out dish rag,
a pin cushion infinitely pricked—
a stubbed toe, the funny bone's compound fracture.
Is it too late to say what I want?
And if it is, there's time still
to want it all the same: this peace
I'm allowed just long enough
for it to be shredded
by the punchline's riot,
that tree rising up a thousand feet.
Only a romantic
would go, as I will go, to tear
it from the earth for ruining scale,
to stand among the roots waiting to be crushed.

Popular Romance

To hum in a smoke-dank alley a song by Elvis
was not the height of my love for you. To turn
my arm from its socket like a hateful thing

was not devotion only. To speak your name
like a spell to my imagined foes was not
peace, no, not ever. Rather, you were a stone

I licked and pretended to eat. You were
ever a dream of falling. An odor of smoke.
You were the design of my worst

crimes. What I stole for love added up.
It added up to nothing. To the air perfumed
by an absent woman. To a box

filled with crushed chalk. God save me
from the stars, once and for all—
I have had enough. Let me love anything

but that: let me go free and dream
of green oceans and the surf
that batters some other world to sleeplessness.

O. It is enough to whisper only
this. To speak to the flame in your breast
and hear nothing else. Once

I believed I could possess
what touched you: the worn sweater,
or the song on the radio

that meant nothing and all in that instant.
Against your door I pressed
my ear, and heard nothing, the whisper

of water, maybe, a breath of cool air—
the gossip of your absence—
and nothing in me could knock or wait,

and all around me the night
spread like water through a rag,
and I let my hands drop whatever they held.

These Arms of Mine

Let's promise never to love like the octopus:
floating in darkness, in jellied ink,
its beak the only hardness it knows,
and though I can't imagine how
it helps matters, in the eight-armed
midst of its mating, a limb
will often fall away from the body,
by ecstasy amputated to the silt.
All morning I've failed to find
why, though no one fails to mention
that death soon follows all
this armlessness. It's fascinating but a mess.
Imagine if each time we kissed
my ear fell off. If the morning
was not so much for brushing
the fog of the night from the mouth,
but reassembly. You might go
out into the day with my bad ankle.
I'd never hear the end.
What would there be to talk about
except that we were falling
apart, and too soon, and how dull
it had all become, this entropy, this shedding,
this habit of the cephalopod
no one can explain. Maybe
it's like the threatened sea cucumber
everting its guts, to leave
less to hunger's hunger. Maybe
eight arms is one arm too many to bear
in the alien instant
of that inscrutable love.

That I would understand, that I could recognize
in the mirror of my skin,
in yours, there in the crushing depth
of the night. There we'd find
each other like exotic gods,
our hands manifold, our fingers infinite—
well, almost. Soon:
the subtraction, the severing, the silence like a wave.

Such as Myself

How can one forget each day to eat *something*
or palm dry gobs of vitamins
or eye the nubile bark of the pink dogwood
burning like adolescence right there
in the miserable scrub of land,
in what no one would call a lawn—
not even the dictionary,
not even the newly born
into this language which trembles
like a rattle. How can one begin
the swim upward, through air,
through the sizzling day,
upward to the moon which is immense
at least to us singing our tiny
songs, each to each and then to no one at all.
And to the bottlebrush throngs
of the oversexed caterpillars
inching their wing-starved lives
towards a mate, towards their alien mating,
how can one make amends
to the living for all the dead
smashed beneath our shadows.
How can one sink in water
and wish to come back
to the reedy bank of the world
that will not pass away,
no matter the apple in the dream,
no matter the girl robed
in rain. How can one answer the choir of crows.

How can one weigh the air
against the gate of glass,
the dew-slick window,
the front door thrumming with the orbit of the days.
How can one turn out
the pockets of his love
and not fear the inventory.
How does one stop
the horizon spinning like a compass.
How does one go on.

Poem for the National Hobo Association Poetry Contest

I will not be there with you but think
of all the misery we've yet
to romanticize. Think of the train cars
rattling all night like the bones
of an epileptic. Think of the song
your mother sang to soap
and how her words drained away
with dirt. Think of the door
that screamed its rusted
warning each time you entered
and the last time you left,
your life knotted up in a red bandana on a stick.
Think of St. Louis, frozen
in April. Think of the girl
who does not know she existed,
that she throbs like a nerve exposed,
that she drains away
each night. I will not be there
to learn your names
or hear of the strange happinesses
beneath the sky
or to swear to return
but think of your feet by a mythic fire warmed
and the orchard around you
pelting the night with apples.
Think of those immense barges
singing like baleen whales
and think of your escapes,
which are legend,
of which I will someday hear.

And thinking of you
in winter the river
speckled with snow
will not be the slab where your body last lay.

Notes for My Body Double

The plot hole by which you must enter in
to the story is a doozy, a real humdinger,
if you will, and it is all made of fire,
the way the stars are made of fire,
though we dream them to be utterly cold
and prickly with a sad light. Nothing
ever stops in my world to hear me
singing to you. I have always loved you,
sweet twin, beloved *doppelgänger*,
alien lump of word in my mouth,
language I spent three years learning
only to forget when it grew too hard
the phrases that meant something:
Dear, I am your long lost butter cookie;
and, *I am sorry, it was accidental,*
but I have dipped the poodle in laudanum.
Let us do away with digression
for the night, though to me
it has always seemed the heart's core,
and think on our motivation
for the lines to follow:
the suddenness of our sorrow is shocking
and the day is hollowed out
and here at this moment,
this crucial hinge of the breaking heart,
I think of the day years ago
when I was a boy and came upon my uncle,
a fish's tail clamped in his teeth,
tearing the skin from the fish with such force
I could hear it—

and I felt so strange and empty
I have never spoken of it
to anyone, or let myself on a day
whole with sun think of it.
What he was doing, and why,
I never asked; there is never
an answer large enough for a world
so huge with meanness.
And I was pulled from myself
but couldn't feel a thing,
and this is your motivation,
mirrored self, speaking back
the words I make wrongly,
lifting the heavy, crude lot of anything
I can't. You must know me
exactly, apart from yourself,
to give back to the world what I can't.
You must know the angles
of light so well the shadows
will accept you like a brother.
You must not choke back my breath
when the ashes on the wind
blind even the birds in the trees.

Questions for Silence

In its first thin tide. In the place
to which it's come like a stranger.
Where the day is a map
you cannot read, crickets begin
in the warm night to whirr
green songs they could not unlearn
had they minds to grow bored.
The willow tree shudders
as though it were sewn up
with twitching nerves, with wire
bright as new-minted pennies. Where
do you go to gain the ear
of the moon, its ravaged face
lamented by no one? And
what do you tell something so old
it cannot remember
being once part of the world and not the sky?
What would your shadow care
to hear, to come close, to touch
hand to wall the tremor
of a passing train? If it had bones inside it,
you know it would flee.
So what are your words worth
to the hurried traffic,
to everything blurred,
to the ice-cream truck
and its sweet patrol,
its song spilling out like a toy,
even in the dark? For all the sunlight
passing from the world

like a thought, who might you sing
to timid sleep? However long
you waited for rain
to rinse you of light's molten color,
for the elbow of the river
to bend back
to your life, the grass whispers
you waited too long
and all the while it speaks
it grows.

For a Woman's Back

The French have a word for the small
of a woman's back, *ensellure,* and God
forgive the poverty of the tongue I was born to.
Whole days have stopped me dead
on my shambling way to the bank or barber
to watch for a time the brocade of rain
streaming from a magnolia's branches.
Homeward I would think of all the ways
to describe to you what I saw.
Love, I thought, for I always begin with love,
the earth owes us this small joy—.
Or, this: Lucifer's wife must be weeping,
and soon I was lost in the tangle
of my childhood, in the speech of my mother,
who would have called that rain
a gullywasher. How quickly I lose my way.
Forgive me. To speak
of one desire is to invite a thousand others
home with you, and by their look
all of them are starved for love and affection
as they purr and tug at your cuffs.
Over there, sharpening her claws
on the refurbished heirloom divan
is the desire to see Prague
just once in its frail blush of spring.
Sprawled on the couch is unrequited love,
pale and wan, forever undone
by countless Keatsian swoons—
he doesn't breathe so much as weepily sigh.
It's better that I keep silent.

end have

So much trouble has taken root in my life
and caught me unaware,
as tonight when crossing the street
I stepped out without a thought for what roared
down upon me, snarling smoke:
nothing. All around me, the night:
as if I were the only one
who had, in all the history of the world,
mattered at all, as if fate
perched upon my shoulder like a chattering bird
and to its precocious song
I ordered my steps. And here I came
alone with just these few words
and this snatch of song looping again
and again. It goes like this—
but you can't hear me, or be touched at all.
In the full moon's face I see
what I've forgotten: each star to be wished on
awash in blankness and my shadow
which stays put like an obedient pet,
no matter how hard I pray to slip out of it,
no matter what I dream.

Ode

In praise of the hermetic sky
which has in all my life never lifted
away to reveal the littered blot of space
like an accusation I can't bear,
not tonight, not when aspirins
spill like bitter white coins
into my palm for my body, for my blood
to spend. In praise of the never
coming morning and the eternally concussed
bird shattering tree bark
with its face so that it might feed—
in praise of the worms, the grubs,
the insignificant life it pierces like a needle.
In praise of raw need. In praise
of the dream of a severed thumb
made of ice, melting away
on the white sun of a stove's cooking eye.
In praise of the next world.
In praise of the most distant object
human history has observed,
that galaxy the first frail vintage of light,
reaching us only now,
like a surprise, like spring, like the early spring
in which you and I, love,
feared for the bulbs rising
from the yard's thawed clod
to the faithless sun of that February.
In praise of the tulip-fed swine of Denmark
and their dead ribs that shed
their meat almost primly

when lifted from the plates you served
to people who knew you,
if only for an hour,
before I did. In praise of those hours
that led here to this instant,
to which I am chained
like a dog. In praise of the fat moon, in praise of my howl.

Perfume

So her hair was a humidor and in it
was tucked every arid vice
I could think of. But in this all
I could do was fail. Little nest,
I'd say, I'd sing, I'd sigh,
while she slept and the world kept on,
there's nothing more
to add to our little pile of change.
And what could we buy
when the night shook
with the mute approach of the stars
like herds of the dead
elephants, whose graves were chalk?
Not a thing. I was poor
in our little bed
and swaddled in sleep
I tried to remember her knee against
mine. Or the gray hum
of the parking garage
that rose up
squat and stupid in raw December air
and, empty, let us
love that we were alone.
Each word into the air
I stirred like water into ink.
In imaginary Chinese I sang
to her sweet throat
bright bird, lost love, where are you now?

Erasure

The word could be more pleasant—
it could be this not-autumn
outside, a cerulean grace above—
and it could be less, it
doesn't bloom in the mouth
like a metal flower,
a meal of fork and not one warm crumb—
and so I'm grateful
even as I slide the film of your face
and mine into a folder
and this folder,
its color the name of an exotic city
in which we never woke,
this folder into a drawer of dust and darkness.
When I was a boy,
one of the infinite fascinations
flowering all
around
was the mothball, poisonous white gumdrop
and weird garrison against
these ragged bits
of flutter that terrified me
at night
on the porch.
I'd think of the deep drifts of sweaters
upon which they desired
to feast, their invisible mouths full of invisible hunger.
And what did mothballs do,
except smell
like one's ancient grandmother,

her ancient breasts
massive with the years?
I never knew.
By my own hands,
you're going away,
piled unto forgetfulness
with the old
things that equate one manner of pain
with another
and I wish there were some better word for it all
but of course
there's not. Through
the phone we once made up vocabularies
and diagrams
best left unsaid
to preserve dim decorum.
The air wavers
with spastic moths
and what they want to eat is all the light.

Poem in Which I Seek Consolation in the Etymology of a Word

Not even in *buxom* could I find solace today,
traipsing backwards through mouth
after mouth, through muck and mire and Middle
English to end in all the words
deemed Old: here in this history
made of air, the word meant *to bend or bow*
before it meant Mae West.

Love, in the pages of this dictionary
you are buxom when you bend
in darkness to send the alarm
backwards to sleep, to slumber, to snooze—
a word this book ignores

utterly. Of all my laments, this
may be the least of them,
but some part of me the world began to call

the heart some thousands of years ago
is grieved by absence
more than you might in all this blue life believe

when I bend my breath like a willow
when I sigh
into the empty mouth of the phone
making a small prayer

to the binary gods of answering machines and voice mail
when I speak my name

to the silent air of your home.

Hunger

Let's eat something no sane person would eat
and in the dark with our zealous fingers
like savages. Each rich subterranean rind
or wheel of cheese we'll pretend
to fluently call forth from greater darkness
than this. Avatars of avarice, open
mouth to sautéed cephalopods
and crusted crustaceans and bivalves over braziers,
let's swell until the dawn
like storm clouds, like stomachs, like stolid
hunger. Once, once upon a time,
once for a friend you served
every manner of meat on a stick.
I forget why. Let's develop
allergies to our allergies,
let's submerge ourselves in intolerable tastes,
let's love the hives and hide
the loaves of bleached white bread
for a year, let's give to the mouthing ducks
down at the filthy brackish pond
all things plain. No valid communion
that does not drip with gluten
the Vatican has voted, even for the devoted few
who will die if they partake
of the host. And no valid communion
for us, love, until we've served
the ramshackle Pope the fried brains of squirrels,
still eaten in time-warped,
blue-grassed Kentucky
where, once upon a time, we did not loll
on the porch nursing mint juleps

but it's a nice thought. Let's add that to the mercurial
menu of our bottomless lives
and let's transcribe our mothers' recipes
into Esperanto, that fake language
that no one speaks.
But this is the language I speak
when I've an appetite for the moon and for you,
both shining like a quarter,
the one asleep in the sky and the other in this bed.

The Numbers Are Not In

The world is filled with those who want
someone else, just as the world
is split in halves, or hemispheres
if we want the word that says it
with a measure of beauty. Most times,
we do. But tonight, what
you get is halves. Tonight
what you get is another unanswered
question. Something like,
why do cyclones spin counterclockwise
in this half of the world?
Something like my thoughts
in the shower, my body
washed by someone else,
and I'm thinking of dark matter,
not because my heart
on its haunches sits bleeding out
like last week's roadkill possum,
its hateful mouth red raw,
but because dark matter is one more thing
I won't ever understand.
No knowledge could I put on
that might plug the holes,
that might seal the chinks
through which my mind goes
after you. When I read
the absurd science
of how we might one day upload our minds,
it's Ted Williams

I'm thinking of:
his severed head
poorly cared for
in its Kelvin crypt of absolute zero,
now cracked, now
the Splendid Splinter even in death.
And it's that wish
I'm thinking of,
to come back better
or new,
to walk out onto the pliant summers
of our best years
when we knew sex to be
as easy, as assured,
as breath.
Love, the dark
that waits, holds
answers like a winning hand
and I've stopped
asking. Whatever I know,
I build it as a bird
builds her fragile bowl of a nest.
And in that nest a bird sings.
Of course,
of course,
she sings to the yolk yellow world inside each blue egg
and for a time,
for as long as I can stand,
I listen.

Love Poem

The hummingbird's jade panic hovering
at the flower's sweet throat
doesn't remind me of you. The clematis
coiling upwards like a plume
of envy does not call to mind your skin,
freckled and far. The jonquils
and their snapped necks are no
emblem of the sun lulling us asleep
in Pinckneyville, Illinois, your favorite town.
No, they are themselves
only. This love poem
is not a love poem. Last week
before winter had relented
the sign someone, somewhere held up
to be ignored did not read
will work for one more love poem
and the nine dolphins dead
on the grit-swept beaches of Florida
didn't mysteriously die
while someone looked on too late
because another day passed
without a rain-glazed lyric
from me. It would be better
if I gave my breath here
to them, but they're gone and all I can do is curse
everything invisible. My heart
is muscle. You've seen it
shudder behind my ribs
as though it too would escape the sea
I hold inside. My heart
isn't a metaphor, not today

and not in this poem
which ignores everything lovely I can see:
the clouds aimless above
and the forms they might suggest
were I to look beyond *cirrostratus* and *cumulonimbus*
and see the cottony dromedary
crossing the cobalt desert
of the sky. He hasn't had a drink
of water for weeks, that beast,
though in the love poem this is not
an oasis is not far
and the branches of trees are burdened by fruit
and in each there is a pit
hard as stone
from which a thousand green groves will someday grow.

Water

How I wanted to graze with my hand
the armored hides of sturgeons
aslosh in their shallow tanks
I did not tell you, nor did I think
to say how the garfish, sentry-like
in their dull brown orbits,
with their pen-shaped snouts skimming food,
were named by someone
who knew that *gar* meant spear
in Old English. I forgot
my place in the story I idly told you,
as we rose in the elevator,
as your hands found in my neck a knot
your fingers could untie
with ease. Love, you know
that language failed me
early with you: in my mouth you found
a hidden stammer. In all
the days since, what have I said
that was right? So little.
But know: when we stood on one side
of thick glass to watch
a world of water ignore our entire lives,
I kissed your fingers
and each one in that light was blue.

Ptolemaic Sunset

It isn't the sun or the sky turbid with rose
light that I'm thinking of, my face
pressed to the glass of the window
as though here I might sleep and dream
of escape. No, I'm thinking
of smoke rising like the inverse of snow
from each table you serve
tonight. I'm thinking of the awful jukebox,
pregnant with the roe of quarters
but no good song. I'm thinking
of the couple that does not quite dance
though with your eyes
you wish them to. I'm thinking of the night
so riddled with stars you swear
the midwestern sky opens to a heaven
we cannot know. I'm thinking
of Ptolemy and his antique earth
mapped as we once were in the middle of all
and the nine heavens he devised,
the last of them devoid of any stars
and home to God where He might shine alone.
I'm thinking of the smile
reflected now in this glass,
the smile I make to the dark
when I speak your name aloud like a question
and you answer without a word.

Lullaby

for Brett

Of salt's place in ancient Roman currency,
paid out in rough burlap bags
to soldiers bearing the weight of empire,
I'll speak for a while tonight.
For as long as I can recall some scrap
of trivia, I'll utter *circa, anno domini,*
I'll trace the bloody lines of Caesars
and serve *garum,* a sauce of fish
left to curdle in the light of that bronze sun,
which I know only as much of
as childhood reading could teach me.
I care even less for it, it must be said, tonight,
while you sleep on the couch,
your body careless and dreaming,
calm, lulled by my invocation
of the useless, the quotidian, the dust-deep
particulars which I've stored
against—what? A winter so long
we forget our names, our numbers,
our address here in this town
that won't do us the sweet favor of fading?
No, there is no reason to know
any of this, to say
not *gesundheit* or *God bless you* or even *yuck*
to the machine gun sneezer
across the dinner table last night
but rather to offer
in perfect serenity to the half-deaf world
the average speed of the human sneeze

as it leaves the nose like a *shinkansen*,
the Japanese word for their hurtling bullet trains.
Which leads me to say how *kamikaze*
means divine wind, a fact I loved
before I loved you. And there I go, rattling
like an old fan. And still you sleep,
small and warm, having asked
in your drowsing slip of a voice
that I talk and talk, quietly, without cease,
about anything, anything at all,
until you drift and I am at last the one you dream of.

Practice

Love, my faith is vague. When others speak
of how they practice it, I think of kung fu
and plywood split by pajamed banshees,
how they always say you learn
such force through practice, pain repeated until
pain isn't pain. It's the piccolo
humming slivers of sound
that won't ever be music
no matter the fervor of practice,
no matter the pursed poise
of your lips. When I write you, when I peel
away the stamps one no longer
need lick, I'm careful. Careful
for ounces of ink and pulp
and minutes shaved from time
if it exists at all and these words
I strung together beyond needful elaboration
only to say I thought of you
today beside the humming fountain
and had no change to wish
you some better life,
some cloud of shade to be
at your infinite beck, your always and immediate
call. A form of faith I follow
is the sky because it never falls,
despite the testimony of chickens
snuffed by hail, ragdolled by the rain
and through my window
I'm watching the last of summer
as the leaves begin to curl

in invisible fire
and I want to tell you
just one thing, it is not urgent,
over and over again.

UNIVERSITY OF NEBRASKA PRESS

Also of interest in the Prairie Schooner Book Prize in Poetry series:

Leopold's Maneuvers
By Cortney Davis

In the venerable tradition of caregivers writing about the healing arts—a tradition peopled by the likes of Anton Chekhov, Walt Whitman, William Carlos Williams, Walker Percy, and Denise Levertov—Cortney Davis brings to poetry the experience, insight, and compassion of a nurse practitioner who daily confronts the unexpected frailties, passions, and power of the flesh.

ISBN: 978-0-8032-6643-8 (paper)

Famous
By Kathleen Flenniken

She "became famous, finally, to herself," Kathleen Flenniken writes. This is the kind of fame at the heart of most lives and at the center of Flenniken's first collection. Here "a little voice sings / from the back of the auditorium / of my throat. Aren't all of us / waiting to be discovered?"

ISBN: 978-0-8032-6924-8 (paper)

Adonis Garage
By Rynn Williams

Adonis Garage introduces a talent exquisitely keyed to the register of New York City's pulse and to the heartbeat of the day. Raw and graphic, with a brash and beautiful voice, Rynn Williams's poetry immerses us in disillusionment and desire and bears witness to the meaning of survival.

ISBN: 978-0-8032-9857-6 (paper)

Order online at www.nebraskapress.unl.edu or call 1-800-755-1105. When ordering mention the code BOFOX to receive a 20% discount.